FaithLeaps

The Christian Mom's Guide to Passion, Purpose, and Profits

Alyssa Avant

Contents

Introduction

Have you ever gotten an idea on your mind and you just couldn't shake it? That is what happened to me with this book. The concept and materials actually started nagging at me in 2009, when I was working from home with my babies in my lap. Much of this book was actually written back then, but has been tweaked over time to become what you hold in your hands today.

I would start writing the book, get stuck, and push the idea to the back of my mind. I wanted desperately to complete it, but just seemed to be stalled. Though the book is just now becoming a reality almost four years later, I believe it is finally what it needed to be all along. Without drawing the process out, many of the things I learned would not be in the book. Therefore, I believe God had a divine plan for everything to take place just as it has. Many of the experiences I have had made this book better than it ever would have been four years ago.

If you're reading this book, it is my prayer that it is a blessing to you. God has a plan for your life and He will work in and through you to complete it in His time. There have been many times over the course of my journey that I wondered how other moms have felt on their journeys. I had never come across a book that gave me the window into another mom's life that I was looking for. Hopefully, FaithLeaps will be that window for you.

And please, let me know when you get published! I'd love to interview you on my website :)

Chapter One

Leap of Faith

My husband and I were sharing a rare moment alone in a hotel room. What was I doing? Reading, as usual. The next words I read stopped me. "If you want to walk on water, you've got to get out of the boat."

The writer challenged me, and I inhaled the next few sentences.

> "Your boat is whatever represents safety and security to you apart from God. Your boat is whatever you are tempted to put your trust in, especially when life gets stormy. Your boat is whatever keeps you from joining Jesus on the waves. Your boat is whatever pulls you away from the high adventure of extreme discipleship. Want to know what your boat is? Your fear will tell you. Just ask yourself this: What is it that

most produces fear in me – especially when I think of leaving it behind and stepping out in faith?" [John Ortberg, *If You Want to Walk on Water*, Grand Rapids, MI: Zondervan, 2001, 17].

I nudged my husband who stared at the television. "Can I read you something?" He turned down the volume. I read him the paragraph and paused. Then, feeling brave, I pressed him. "What do you think my boat is?"

He answered without hesitation. "The church."

His prompt answer surprised me. Before you become skeptical or consider me a hypocrite, allow me to explain. At that time, I was Youth and Children's Director at a local church. He believed my position there was my "boat," and, after a moment of thought, I agreed. It was comfortable, secure, and did not require me to put a great deal of faith in God on a daily basis. For several years, I had done the job well and it came easy for me. I felt secure in the position I held and in my abilities.

In those days of working part-time in ministry, I knew exactly how much income was coming into our home each month. I calculated it to the penny. So the church had also become my boat because it provided financial security. In his book, *Crazy Love*, Francis Chan explains, "We like finding refuge in what we already have rather than in what hope God will provide."

If God had not nudged me, urged me, and maybe even pushed me into my leap of faith, I would not be where I am today. That hotel-room conversation was one of those nudges. Not long afterward, I resigned from my comfortable position in the ministry and began pursuing my calling. God called me out of the boat, out of my comfort zone, and into a different life.

I did not realize, until those changes began to take place, how deeply my faith could run. Sure, I trusted God from day to day, but I did not focus on His provision and presence in my everyday life as much as I could have. Four years later, not a day goes by that I do not see the intricate details God has orchestrated to make my life what it is.

I rely on God monthly just to make ends meet. Many times I'd rather do something drastic to find a way to make things work rather than wait on God. Sometimes I battle unbearable doubt, anxiety, and fear. I repeatedly wonder, "Why not just get a job?" As I stare at my computer screen or out the window, I wonder, "How will this ever work out?" However, I now have story after story of how God met and exceeded my needs every time. He has never failed me.

What Is Faith?

Faith is unlike anything else you will do or feel in life. It takes a long time to understand, and your feelings may take a long time to catch up. As the Bible says, "Faith is being sure of what you hope for and certain of what you cannot see" (Hebrews 11:1 NIV).

Faith begins with a relationship with Jesus Christ, the Man who gave everything - - even His own life-- for our sins.

Why do we need faith in the first place? Some may ask.

Yet others think we can never have enough faith. *It takes a great deal of faith to accomplish something and I just don't know that I believe that strongly.*

Remember the promise made in the gospel of Matthew. We may think that it takes a great deal of faith to accomplish something; however, the Bible assures us, "If you have faith as small as a mustard seed, you can say to this mountain, 'Move from here to there,' and it will move. Nothing will be impossible for you" (Matthew 17:20 NIV).

Do you ever feel that nudge to take action, but then hesitate? Taking a leap of faith is scary. Ask yourself: what leap of faith do I need to take?

12

What is a faith leap?

A faith leap is stepping out of your own comfort zone into the hands of God. I learned this firsthand, after taking my own leap of faith five years ago. One critical element of a faith leap is having enough faith to take the first step, whether you take it trembling or firmly planted with confidence. Either way, you must take the step!

The Call

I grew up in church and had a faith-saturated life. I had heard about being "called" many times. I watched fellow church members walk the aisle and make a commitment to ministry. Some accepted a call to a foreign country to share Jesus as a missionary, whether for a short time or for a lifetime. Others felt called to become a pastor or to serve in youth ministry.

As I grew older, I encountered people who felt "called" and who had stepped out by faith and done something new, whether it was starting a new ministry at church, speaking on a topic about which they were passionate, or writing on their own hot topic through a blog. I discovered there was no singular definition for having a "calling" from God-- no two callings were ever quite the same.

No matter how others defined God's call, I still felt it in my life when I walked the aisle in church and committed my life to full time Christian service. At 18, I assumed that could only mean ministry inside the walls of the church. I have since served in ministry in a local church for just over five years of my life professionally, and for many more years as a volunteer.

When I felt called, I couldn't pinpoint a specific direction for my calling. This made my decision process, as far as what areas of ministry to pursue, more difficult.

Have you ever felt this way? Have you questioned your calling? Have you asked yourself, "Am I really being called to speak, to write, to do ministry, or to pursue business when I do not know what that means and I'm not even clear on what exactly I am being called to do?"

The business portion did not become a reality for me for many years, because I didn't realize God might actually call me to a business. However, I do believe the answer is yes. *Yes*! We can be called even if we do not know all the details.

God is clear in His Word. He calls us and He equips us. However, sometimes He isn't clear on exactly where He is taking us or how quickly He will get us there.

Our calling is not like a flight to another location, where we know the detailed itinerary. It is a clarion call, a summons to go forth. Most likely, God will not give us all the details up-front. He doesn't usually work that way. Instead, He gives us the information bit by bit, as we rely on Him in faith. That's why it's called faith. We can be sure that God calls each one of us to something. He puts a passion inside us, deposits dreams, equips us with the necessary abilities.

He also bestows spiritual gifts upon us that become ours at the time we accept His Son Jesus as Savior. All we must do to use those gifts is to receive the gift of salvation that comes from Jesus when we acknowledge Him as our Savior and Lord. (We will discuss these things further in chapter two.)

"There are different kinds of gifts, but the same Spirit. There are different kinds of service, but the same Lord. There are different kinds of working, but the same God works all of them in all men" (1 Corinthians 12:4-6 NIV).

To determine our calling from God, we must have a relationship with Him. We must spend time with Him and allow Him to speak to us. Though we may not know what God calls us to do, He can, and will, speak to us.

Some practices that helped me to understand my call:

Pray

Prayer is our form of communication with God. How better to know if God is calling us than to ask Him? He wants to hear from us. He will answer us. Though the answer may not be what we want to hear, nor as soon as we want to hear it, He will answer in His time and in His way. Take the time to seek Him and His answers through prayer.

We might also seek the help of a prayer partner to lift us up in prayer as we sense a particular call on our life. We can often discern the direction God is giving us more easily through the confirmation or correction of wise counsel.

Listen

After praying, the next step is to listen. We cannot hear God speaking if we do not take time to be quiet and listen to him. This can be difficult for some of us but it is absolutely necessary. How can we hear His call, if we don't make time to hear Him?

As we listen, we will hear that "still small voice."

Gut check

Yes, take a moment and do a gut check. Many times that feeling in the pit of our stomachs let us know something is off, or on the positive side, that something simply *must* happen. God places that feeling there. Some might call it our conscience; others refer to it as intuition. Some would say the feeling in their stomach comes from the Holy Spirit. Whatever we call the message from our "gut," whether it feels like happy butterflies or cold fear, it can help us to discern God's call.

Circumstances

God confirms or denies what we may believe to be true often through the circumstances in our lives. He can use those things to help alert us and to spur us to action.

Seek God's face

Above all else, let God know that you are seeking Him. Talk to Him often, consult His Word, worship Him, and thank Him. Commit your life to Him whether your calling is to speaking, writing, ministry, business, or something different.

"But seek first his kingdom and his righteousness, and all these things will be given to you as well" (Matthew 6:33 NIV).

Are you unsure of the calling God has placed on your life? Are you aware of your God-given passions and purpose? Whether the answer is yes or no, I pray you will continue with me as we discuss passions and purpose.

Chapter Two

Find Your Passion

Do you remember Christmas morning back when you were a small child? That giddy, anxious feeling of wanting to jump straight out of bed to discover what the day had in store, and even more importantly--what gifts were under the tree? Perhaps you would find a shiny red bike complete with a bell, or a baby doll with sparkling eyes and golden blond hair!

My father loved Christmas morning as much as my brother and me. As soon as we waltzed into his bedroom and announced that Santa came, he would jump out of bed and hurry with us to the tree. Even though he already knew every detail of the gifts, he patiently listened as my brother and I described each one. Then, he opened and assembled every dollhouse, rocket ship, and puzzle we received. The hours multiplied as we sat on the living room floor and savored our goodies. My father loved every minute of our childhood, especially those glorious Christmas mornings. Today, he still basks in the joy of Christmas as he interacts with his grandchildren.

Our Heavenly Father has this same joy and passion for His children and the gifts, talents, abilities, and passions that He placed into each of our lives. Just like my father, He longs to jump out of bed each morning and sit with us as we open, assemble, and work with the instructions He has given us. Much like attempting to put together a complicated toy, we have the opportunity to sit with our Father and decipher the steps on our path.

Living my passion each day as an entrepreneur has in many ways taken the place of the excitement I felt as a child over my brand new toys.

What Is Passion?

Have you read a brilliant book or seen a riveting movie lately? Did it trigger any emotion in you? Did you wind up mentioning it to your friends as a result? This is similar to how passion works. We do not tire of talking about something that holds considerable interest for us. Unlike a movie or book, however, we don't lose interest in our life passion even after we've talked about it for a while. If we have a passion for something, it will be very easy for us to write a fairly extensive list of things we know about the subject.

According to Dictionary.com, passion is a noun meaning *any powerful or compelling emotion or feeling.* When we're passionate about something, we feel such powerful emotions toward it that we cannot help but talk about it and promote it, even if we don't get anything in return. What are you passionate about? Maybe praying for your children, helping single mothers get the assistance they need, or teaching teenagers how to deal with peer pressure? The possibilities are endless. Your passion is unique to you. Though others may be passionate about the same thing you are, there is no one else who can pursue that passion the way you can. Have you defined your particular passion yet? Don't worry, we'll work first, to uncover your passion, and then develop it into a platform which you can use to create a ministry or build a business. If you have already identified your passion, list everything you know about that topic. It will be most helpful if you list those things in two categories, which fall within the area of your passion and experience.

Recently, I attended a workshop by Michelle Prince, the best-selling author of *Winning in Life Now.* In her *Book Bound* Workshop, Michelle led us through an exercise that helped us explore our passions and experience. This simple exercise can help you as well. Divide a blank sheet of paper into two sections. At the top of the first section, write the question, "What am I passionate about?" At the top of the second section, write the question, "What am I good at doing?"

You will then want to write your answers. The following is my actual list from the workshop.

What am I passionate about?

- Speaking
- children
- learning
- DIY
- helping others
- leading
- entrepreneurship
- my faith
- business
- personal development
- manners/etiquette

What am I good at doing?

- Technology
- teaching
- planning
- encouraging
- organizing
- writing
- encouraging my children to be independent
- motivating children / teenagers

There is a space at the end of this chapter where you can do this exercise now. Go ahead, then return here and continue reading.

The Narrow Road

After listing these things, we can narrow down what we are most passionate about by comparing the two lists. *What is it that you are both passionate about and good at doing?* Where these two items intersect is where you will find the topic or topics which will direct your journey to fulfillment. Look to find which things you know the most about *and* which you are able to share with others.

Next, write down everything you already know about the particular topic where you found that intersection. An extensive list of your qualifications will give you confidence to begin your journey.

What if I still cannot identify my passion?

Don't worry, we're about to dig deeper.

We are going to take two tests. Don't stress out! They aren't the graded kind. These tests will help you to learn more about yourself and where your passion might lie. We are going to explore both your personality and your spiritual gifts. God created all of us as humans in His image. The Bible says it this way: "So God created man in his own image, in the image of God he created him; male and female he created them" (Genesis 1:27 NIV). As a part of this, God made each of us unique.

The Bible also gives us the picture in David's words

> "For you created my inmost being; you knit me together in my mother's womb. I praise you because I am fearfully and wonderfully made; your works are wonderful, I know that full well. My frame was not hidden from you when I was made in the secret place. When I was woven together in the depths of the earth" (Psalm 139:13-15 NIV).

God made us unique and intricate. We are complicated human beings, and a part of the place we see that complexity is in our personalities. Though there are similarities among personalities, we are all different and uniquely made.

Since there are no two of us exactly alike, we each have something to share that no one else does. Do not be intimidated by others who may share what you consider to be your passion.

Explore Your Personality

I encourage you to take time now to explore your personality, perhaps by using one of the many personality tests available on the Internet today. As a psychology major, my experience studying personality goes back many years. I have experience with many different types of surveys. That is why I enjoy studying the materials of Florence Littauer, author of a series of books on personality including *Personality Plus: How to Understand Others by Understanding Yourself.*

You can find a free personality assessment based on her book at http://www.gotoquiz.com/personality_plus_1. Take a few moments now to take that quiz and reflect on your own God-given personality.

From the test, we see that there are four personality types, which lend themselves to different passions and gifts.

According to Littauer's book, *Your Personality Tree*, the four personality types are Sanguine, Choleric, Melancholy, and Phlegmatic. Each of these personality types has specific traits and both strengths and weaknesses.

Littauer describes these personality types the following way: The Sanguine is the *talker,* the Choleric is the *worker*, the Melancholy is the *thinker*, and the Phlegmatic is the *watcher*. Knowing our personality, along with its strengths and weaknesses, can help us to understand others and ourselves better, as Littauer suggests.

Our gifts complement our personality but are not the same thing. We are each skilled in doing certain things, and these are called our talents. Our talents and our gifts are also similar but not identical.

When we think of talents, we often think of the ability to play a sport well, or being musically inclined. Spiritual gifts, on the other hand, lend themselves to Biblical concepts such as teaching, preaching, serving, and others.

Exploring the Gifts

Gifts, in a physical sense and in a spiritual sense, are different. Spiritual gifts are those God gives us that we do not necessarily deserve. I believe that spiritual gifts are given to us as believers at our time of *salvation,* or when we accept Jesus. God then works out these gifts in our lives enabling us to do what He calls us to do. Likewise, our spiritual gifts allow us and give us another means by which to worship or bring glory to God.

Spiritual gifts are different from physical talents in that they are given to us at our time of salvation and are fulfilled supernaturally. Through God's power, not our own, we are able to carry out His work. Physical talents often give us the ability to do things on our own apart from God, but spiritual gifts we cannot use separate from God.

We all know people who do not profess to be Christians who use their natural talents for their own success, money, etc. They do this even though they do not have a relationship with Jesus Christ. With spiritual gifts, this would never be possible. Spiritual gifts only manifest within our relationship with God, and are used to ultimately bring glory to Him. This being said, many times our passions come from our spiritual gifts.

In order to understand and explore your gifts more, I encourage you to take the following Spiritual Gifts Analysis on the web. Then think about your spiritual gifts and determine how you can use them in your life.

The survey is located at http://www.churchgrowth.org/analysis/intro.php. Click on "Free Spiritual Gifts Analysis for Individual Users." For further research on this subject, I recommend that you read the following Scripture passages: 1 Corinthians 12, Romans 12, and Ephesians 4.

Now that we have explored your personality and your spiritual gifts, I encourage you to spend some time in prayer and meditation. Specifically, consider how your personality, your spiritual gifts, and your natural abilities, can lead you to your passion.

Ask yourself:
- What are my spiritual gifts?
- Am I utilizing my God-given gifts?
- How can I make better use of my gifts?

If you already suspect what your passion is, the optimum outcome of your answers will affirm it. If you weren't sure, perhaps you have a better idea. If you were totally clueless, I hope that you are now on the path to uncovering your passion.

Finally, are you ready to make the decision to follow your passion and purpose?

It is your turn. Do the exercise on the next page:

What am I passionate about?

What am I good at doing?

Chapter Three

Choosing a Lifestyle of Passion and Purpose

"I really don't ever want to have a job that won't allow me to be with him," I gushed at my husband.

Tears dripped down my cheeks as feelings of anxiousness swarmed my body. I looked at the tiny baby lying in the nearby bassinet and my chest began to feel heavy. At the time, I didn't know if the church where I worked would allow me to bring my baby to work or if I would have to consider part-time daycare.

The first time I held my babies in my arms, I knew I couldn't be away from them for extended periods. Even now, when they are ages four, five, and nine, my heart aches when I have to leave them for more than a few hours.

We were extremely blessed that the church had no issue with me bringing my baby to work with me. He spent mornings in a playpen in my office and many afternoons, especially in the summer, surrounded by the youth and children of the church.

One summer I paid a youth boy to watch my toddler upstairs at church while I held a children's activity downstairs. I chuckle to this day at the youth's explanation of how he kept my son quiet. He said, "Every time he cried, I'd give him a cookie." My boy may have gotten a few extra cookies that summer, but he was only a few steps away from me at all times.

Your Sweet Spot

Just prior to my second child's birth, I made the difficult decision to resign from my ministry position to work from home. Do you remember that hotel room story in Chapter One? That occurred a year before I resigned.

I had been speaking and writing on the side for several years. The opportunities had become more frequent and I continued to feel God nudging me forward. As I shared in the beginning of the book, this was quite a leap of faith for me.

The same weekend of the hotel room conversation, I had spoken at a mother/daughter retreat and described to my husband the rush I felt when standing before those young girls and their mothers. This was my sweet spot. As I will share with you in Chapter Six, this is exactly where you want to be.

Many times, in order to find our sweet spot, we must take a faith leap. Choosing to pursue a passion and purpose is a pursuit unlike anything else. It is vastly different from doing odd jobs to make ends meet financially.

We are about to explore what it means to choose to be a Christian mom who pursues her passion and purpose and ultimately to profit from it. Making that choice always begins with a "faith leap."

We must decide if we are willing to step out in faith to pursue our sweet spot. Or, we can decide to stay in the comfort of working for someone else or be a mom who has put her dreams aside.

Ultimately, Christian moms must decide, "What do we want?" We must commit to some things if we choose to pursue our passion and purpose.

Be Willing to Commit

Commitment #1 – Be willing to take risks.
God does not promise us that following His path for our lives will be risk-free; however, He does promise us that He has a plan.

"God planned something better for us so that only together with us would they be made perfect" (Hebrews 11:40 NIV).

My biggest risk was that first faith leap: the decision not to work outside the home. It will probably mean something different for you.

We may need to take other risks when we pursue our passion and purpose. We may risk being rejected or questioned by our friends who do not understand. Grow accustomed to the fact that not everyone will be open to or understand what you choose to do.

We may risk a steady paycheck. For me, taking my faith leap meant giving up a consistent income.

Over five years on the other side of my faith leap, I can now share that God's provision has trumped any steady income, many times providing *more* than my comfortable, predictable income.

We may risk loss as we choose to invest in our passion and purpose, whether monetarily or time-wise. We must ask ourselves, "How much are we willing to risk as we seek the passions and purpose God has placed within us?"

Commitment #2 – Be willing to set goals.

It is one thing to pursue one's passion and purpose, but it's an entirely different scenario to pursue one's passion and purpose and, ultimately, to profit from it.

The reality is that we all need money to live. Therefore, often a perk of pursuing our passion and purpose is that we can profit from it. We can then use those profits to supplement our family's livelihood. The joy of the situation is that you can have your cake (your passion and purpose) and eat it too (benefit from it).

Profits (whether financial or otherwise) don't come without commitment. One necessary commitment to make is to set goals. In Chapter Four, we will talk more specifically about goal setting, but just know that setting goals is part of the commitment necessary in order to pursue passion and purpose and, ultimately, profit from it.

One of my goals has always been to write a book. Therefore, with the publication of this book I am achieving that goal. As you continue reading, begin to think about what some of your goals are.

Commitment #3 – Be willing to juggle motherhood and the pursuit of your passion and purpose.

The reason I do what I do is twofold. First, I want to be present in my children's everyday lives. Second, I want to pursue my God-given passion and purpose. Therefore, I must be willing to juggle the two things. Choosing to pursue one's passion and purpose while continuing to be the primary caregiver for your children takes quite a bit of juggling. For me, routines, systems, and schedules have become a way of life in order to maintain both a home for my children and a place for my passion and purpose to thrive.

If you're ready to make these commitments and face this journey head on, let's tackle the next hurdle – keeping all the balls in the air.

Chapter Four

The Balancing Act

When I first started my work-from-home journey, I was the mother of a newborn baby and a toddler. People constantly asked me, "How do you do it?" At the time, *it* meant the normal everyday routine that comes with a toddler and a newborn: feedings, numerous diaper changes, naps, baths, plus all the usual housework, as well as business work. I had just begun my ghostwriting business. Between the diaper changes and feedings, I wrote many articles on any number of topics. The baby's nap time sure came in handy!

A topic I researched on Google was the word "balance." I desperately wanted a way to find more hours in my days. I found what claimed to be the "ticket" to a more balanced life, advice from time management gurus to daily planners that promised more than they could ever deliver.

The truth is, there is no way humanly possible to obtain more than 24 hours in each day that God gives us.

Is Balance a Reality?

From my experience of close to five years of working from home and rearing three children under the age of nine, I have discovered that balance is, at best, a myth. If you have too much on your plate, one area will suffer as a result of another area taking up too much of your time. One person cannot do more than there is time for in a day.

I have always been a little unrealistic about what I could do each day. Blame it on my over-achiever personality or my workaholic tendencies, but whatever the case, I soon learned that I could not get everything I wanted to done in a day.

This is why determining your priorities is so important.

Determining Your Priorities

Priorities are the order of importance which we bestow upon the different areas of our lives. Just recently, I have listened to training materials about life and time management. A truth that I have heard in each of these trainings is that mothers who work at home cannot compartmentalize their lives. Our lives are one big puzzle and all of the puzzle pieces must fit together. If not, the picture of life is distorted and has little to no value.

We must give appropriate attention to God, our spouse, children, ourselves, our homes and our businesses. Most people struggle as one area demands more attention than the others.

For me, this is often my business, because my business is based on my passion and strengths. I enjoy it, and my determined personality leaves me yearning to do more and more. As a result, I tend to neglect other areas, mainly those things I don't enjoy as much, such as laundry, cleaning toilets, or mopping floors. *Can anybody relate?* This can cause strife in our family, so I often have to do a reality check and re-prioritize.

When setting priorities, be honest and realistic with yourself. Your life will never be perfect, and perfect balance can never truly occur. However, there are ways to get a better grip upon your daily life. One tried and tested way that many people have found to work is routines. Creating a set of routines for yourself and your family to follow can help a great deal.

Establishing Routines

Many times people confuse routines with schedules and frown on them, because they don't like the idea of scheduling. Remember when you first had a baby? That little bundle of joy had his or her own routine. Eat and sleep, change, play, eat and sleep, repeat over and over. It kept you on your toes. A routine does that. It keeps you on your toes, and it keeps you moving forward.

My daily routine is the same during my children's school year, but can change slightly during the summer or around the holidays.

My basic daily routine looks like this:

6:45   Rise, shower and dress
7:00   Get children up and dressed for school
7:35   Take children to school
8:00   Arrive back home, breakfast, and Bible reading time
9:00   Check email, check in on social media
10:00 Work
11:15 Pick up my son from pre-school
11:30 Lunch
12:30 Check back in with work related emails, projects
1:30   Clean up, prep dinner
3:00   Pick up older children from school

3:30   After-school snacks, cooking dinner etc.

That's a basic day. Supper follows, and then family time with possibly some work for me squeezed in during the evenings. The most important part of my routine is that it is flexible. This may look like a schedule to you and, broadly speaking, it is. However, built into each area of my day, or time slot, if you will, is a set of routines that I practice. During the morning breakfast time, I read my Bible. After my Bible time, I always head straight to the kitchen to unload the dishwasher from the last load that was run the previous day. I also put in a load of laundry, which I will swap and fold later in the day.

During our clean up time each afternoon, I prep dinner. This means I decide which of the meals we will have from my menu plan, which is another one of my routines. Weekly, I make a menu plan as well as a grocery list as a part of my weekly routine. My menu plan is a list of meals that we will have for the following week. I also have a specific day that I grocery shop so that I don't need to run to town every day for errands, but do it on a weekly basis instead.

The routines that I have in my life have become second nature, but sometimes they do change. One of my favorite benefits of working from home is the flexibility. If one of my children is sick, I can ignore my routines for at least part of the day.

They do, however, serve as a loose guide for my days. Your ability to be flexible will make for much less stress in your life. Other work-at-home moms agree with me about routines. Here is one of their comments:

"I get more done when I stick to a routine. I stay on schedule by having alarms on my phone to tell me when to do certain tasks. It helps to remind me to do the jobs and keeps me on task." (Christie Jarvis, http://christiejarvis.com)

Daily routines are essential for children, especially when they're young. The savvy work-at-home mom will use structure to her advantage so that everyone in the family will know what to expect during the course of the day. For the best results, it's wise to pay attention to natural patterns. For instance, down times, active play, lunch, and naps can all be scheduled when the children naturally tend to be quiet, active, hungry, or tired. The key is to keep the schedule close to the same each day to build familiarity and automatic compliance.

Of course, it's great to allow for spontaneity -- that's what being a kid all is about! Spontaneity is great when it is built into the framework of a basic routine. However, I find my greatest frustrations arise when I expect my children to give *me* space when I've already pushed the limits of *their* patience by not providing a timely snack or by delaying the two-year-old's naptime. Establishing and respecting boundaries work both ways.

"Keeping a balance of fun within the routine takes some forethought, but is definitely worth the effort. Life will be the better for it." (Stephanie Ray, Founder, New Life Balance for Women, http://newlifebalanceforwomen.com)

As Stephanie so adequately explains, routines are important, but must be kept by both the children and the mothers. Even with flexibility, we must stick to them in some form, if they are to serve their purpose.

People who work at home answer only to themselves (ourselves!) and, for some, to clients. Tasks must be done and projects ultimately need to be completed. This takes discipline. John Maxwell, author of *Today Matters*, says, "Good decisions + daily discipline = a masterpiece of potential." He also says that, "the bookends of success are starting and finishing. Decisions help us start. Discipline helps us finish." If we desire success, we must embrace discipline.

In addition, we all know that when we work, and work hard, we will get the itch to play and that's all right. Learn to play. Fit playtime into your day. This is easy for women with young children because they usually demand our attention and a bit of play time each day. My children enjoy an afternoon in the sun, writing with chalk on the sidewalk or going for a walk.

Any work-at-home mom whose big *why* is her family, especially her children, will tell you that juggling the many areas of her life is worth it to lead the life she desires. My lifestyle is one that involves my children in my daily life. As a work-at-home mom you must decide what is right for you. My children do not go to daycare. They are here with me. Interruptions by them are part of my day. Yes, sometimes this is frustrating and there are days I don't feel I get much accomplished. But, I must remember I am at home primarily for my children; my business is not my top priority. Only you can decide what is best for you and your family. If this lifestyle is one which you seek, keep reading as we cover standing firm even when you get the urge to "just go get a job."

Chapter Five

Why Not Just Get a Job?

"Why don't you just get a job?" The question rang in my ears, but I refused to hear it. Other times it would sink in and I would feel sick. Why don't they understand this is what God has called me to do, at least for now?

I always feel offended when someone asks me when I'm going to get a job. I think the first time I ever felt validated in the pursuit of my passion by someone else, was when my father did it. We were on the phone discussing the idea of me having or getting a job and he said to me, "Alyssa, you have a job. You're a writer, a speaker, and a business owner." I could have cried. I think I did, after we got off the phone. It meant the world to me that my daddy saw that I had a job and was proud of me.

Now, back to the well-meaning others who asked that question of me so many times and continue to do so. I must admit that I have even asked myself many times in despair, "Why not just get a job?" I've even followed through with it and taken action before. I have gone so far as to land a J-O-B, and then turn it down. I knew in my heart that I wasn't supposed to take the position, and the cold hard facts were that the job would not have profited me or my family, financially or otherwise.

The job would have meant my being away from my children, with two children in school and one in daycare. It would have meant buying new clothes and filling my van with gas every few days. It would have meant spending over half my paycheck each month on daycare, gas, and the other expenses that the J-O-B would have brought. It would have meant giving up my passions and my time with my children. Maybe it looked like a good idea, but I didn't think so upon closer inspection. Other people in my life thought I should have taken it, and that is all right. They are entitled to their opinions. I call them the naysayers.

The Naysayers

Many times, naysayers are those closest to you: your parents, your best friend, maybe even your spouse. You see, recently I had a revelation. It became clear to me that my best friend, who always told me to get a job, didn't know what else to tell me. I would go to her when money was tight or I was worrying, and ask her for advice. With a long time J-O-B lifestyle, she told me the only thing she knew to tell me, "Go get a job."

We recently had a conversation about this topic, and she admitted her frustration with me over those discussions. She would sense my disappointment and even my frustration or resentment. She'd be equally frustrated because she didn't know what else to say. In her mind, getting a job was the answer.

Let's examine this for a moment.

Consider Your Mindset

There are two schools of thought about taking outside employment. Mine was, and is, that working from home as I do is my calling. Her mindset was and is that a regular job is the answer. Both mindsets make sense. Both are valid and we must choose which we will embrace as ours.

I made up my mind long ago that the work-at home-lifestyle was right for me and that this chosen lifestyle is my God-given calling. You must decide for yourself. Will this lifestyle be difficult? Yes. Would working a regular J-O-B be difficult? Yes. Life is not easy, no matter which lifestyle we choose. The Bible tells us that life on this earth has its share of troubles. Scripture says, "I have told you these things, so that in me you may have peace. In this world you will have trouble. But take heart! I have overcome the world" (John 16:33 NIV).

The first step to ignoring the question, "Why not just get a job?" is to make up your mind. The second is to decide that the lifestyle you chose is the one for you, and then pursue it relentlessly. How do you decide? Think back over your life, your dreams. What has God always nudged you towards? What have you gotten excited about? What has your subconscious told you in your dreams? What is your biggest dream? Have you experienced one particular dream several times? Does your dream invade your waking hours? God has placed that dream inside of you, and it's okay to follow it.

Your Biggest Dream

My biggest dream is coming true right now, as I sit writing this book. I must admit it feels a bit different to do it than I thought it would. It's not nearly as glamorous as I imagined, as I sit here in my pajamas, barefooted, and with a bed head.

However, the truth is, one of my biggest dreams has always been to write a book.

Your dream is probably related to the person you are inside. There is some topic or cause that is important to you. Telling others about this could be your mission. *Am I right?*

Remember, your passion is that thing which you would do whether or not you got paid for it. It's what drives you. This will fuel your mission.

I've always been fascinated with passion and purpose and finding those two things in my own life. Can I tell you how many books I've read on the subject? I have always desired to pursue my passion and my guess is, if you're reading this book, you desire to pursue yours too.

Now, for Christian moms, there is another element to this. The work-at-home lifestyle means not only are we pursuing our God-given passion or purpose, but a part of that purpose is to be a *mom*. If you choose the work- at-home lifestyle, you can pursue your passion and be a full-time mom at the same time. Again, this does not come without its share of difficulties.

I shared with you in Chapter Three how I felt about being away from my children. God knew I'd feel this way. He knows you feel this way, too, because He put that feeling inside of you. He gave you those desires you have. Therefore, we must trudge on in pursuit of our passion and purpose, and ultimately, we will find peace.

That peace is what you seek, *right?* Finding your passion and purpose and pursuing it 100% is the ultimate way to find God's peace because that is how He wired you to be and He is the only one who can bring you that peace.

"Peace I leave with you; my peace I give you. I do not give to you as the world gives. Do not let your hearts be troubled and do not be afraid" (John 14:27 NIV).

I wanted to share with you some stories of how others identified their dream or passion, and how it turned into something they could profit from.

My good friend, *Latara Ham-Ying* shares her story:

"I have always been an entrepreneur at heart. When I was a little girl I would design stores from my mother's jewelry boxes and use her mini-perfume bottles as products for my Barbie Dolls. While my mother never let me go door to door selling candy bars, I knew how many boxes I needed her and my family to sell in order to raise enough money to always be a top seller. Yes, business was in my blood.

"As an adult, having a child at 23 made me realize that I did not want to work outside of the home. I wanted to be home. That is when I opened my day care with only two children. Soon that day care flourished to over twelve children, with an assistant and even a part-time security guard to help keep an eye on the kids as they played outside. When I had to close my daycare it was devastating but necessary at the time. That is when I went back into the world of working out of the home in the corporate field. I loved working out of the home because I loved what I did as a customer service relations expert.

"However, marrying in 2002 brought me back home and I found myself not liking being a stay-at-home mom. I wanted to do more because I knew that being a mother was a role it was who I was. It was a part of the call on my life but not the entire call. So I started searching and soon found myself writing for pay for print and online publications. That was in 2004. In 2006 I branched out into authority blogging and that is when so much changed. I ended up working where I was not supposed to be and I was miserable. I was a VA and while that is a great work at home for some, it was not for me. But I had been discouraged from going for my dreams by coaches and others who said that my dream of a women's ministry online would never work.

"You know what? In a way they were right. They were right because I did not know the true potential of my passions or the purpose for which Integrated Woman Ministries would be birthed. You see, I wanted to be the African-American Beth

Moore. You know, speaking to the heart of a woman. Helping her to heal from pain and come out of depression. Little did I know that God would use that very thing and take it to a whole new arena with the work-at-home woman!

"My call is to be a vessel of transformation; that is a given. But my mission at this time in my walk is to help the work-at-home woman to build her business, brand herself in a godly and professional manner, and learn to be the very woman that God designed her to be. That is my passion. I love helping women realize dreams and walk out the vision.

"I took a tiny leap in 2009 when I started my ministry on a small scale. I was still seeing the dollar signs of the $2000-plus a month I was making as a Social Media VA. I was so laser focused I was no good to the vision God had for me. In 2010 I changed the name of the ministry to Integrated Woman Ministries and taking that step took me for a spin as I witnessed God take away all of my income and ask me what was I going to do next. He told me I was not going in deep enough. It was all or nothing at all. In January 2011, I opened up the membership option of IWM and was shocked at what I found!"

Jenny Deramo of ThePeacefulHousewife.com discovered how she could run a business online.

The Peaceful Housewife began as a blog in order to give Jenny an opportunity to share her love for Christ, parenting ideals, homemade household cleaner recipes, and bargains with anyone who would listen. In only nine months, it has blossomed into a one-stop blog, featuring activities to do with your children, guest posts from national experts, a close-knit community, and many review and giveaway opportunities.

Jenny opened shop and began selling her cleaners when customers began asking her if she would make and sell the homemade household cleaners she talked about and posted recipes for on her blog. Her products and customer service have all received rave reviews from customers and fellow bloggers.

This business model allows Jenny to share her passion and love for Christ on a regular basis while also meeting the needs of thousands of people around the world through her candid blog posts and products. She loves being able to work from home and allow her children to be part of her business. It has provided new income and has given her the fulfillment of knowing that she is pursuing her passions while being present in her children's lives.

You too can find the path God has for you. You have God-given talents, skills, and abilities that He wants you to share with the world. Perhaps ask yourself, "What are they?"

Chapter Six

Capitalize on Your Skills

As I sat there, my grandmother asked what I was reading. I told her that the book was on spiritual gifts. She joked with me that it was Christmas break and asked why I was studying. She asked me if I was tired of studying after all those college exams.

"This is something I'm interested in, which makes it not feel like studying," I remarked.

That's how much I love studying spiritual gifts. I could always get excited about them.

Remember how I encouraged you in Chapter One to take a spiritual gifts assessment? I hope you did.

What are your spiritual gifts? Teaching, exhortation, shepherding, serving, giving, mercy, or perhaps administration? Now consider another type of gift that God has given each of us: our talents. What is the difference?

Gifts versus Talents

Spiritual gifts, as we covered in Chapter Two, are given to us by God for work in His Kingdom. These gifts we receive at the time of our salvation. Talents, though given to us by God, will not necessarily be used for God.

We all know people who have natural talents or abilities: singing, athleticism, great strength or endurance. Many people have talent, which they may or may not choose to use for God. God-given spiritual gifts we are able to use only because of His presence in us and His work in our lives. This is the difference between spiritual gifts and natural talents. We can use both to pursue passion, purpose, and profits, but as I have already mentioned, we must first be aware of what they are.

Explore Your Skills

We want to also be aware of any skills (learned abilities) we possess. A skill is something that we can practice and learn. For example, I possess the skills of web design, typing, and organizing.

As a young girl, I wanted to learn to play the piano. I can recall hours of scale practice in the early days of lessons and practice. It didn't feel as though I would ever learn to play when I could only peck out a few notes at a time.

But, the practice paid off and I recall the joy I felt when I was able to play my favorite hymns beautifully and was even privileged to play in church a few times. Skills are worth the time it takes to develop them.

Ultimately, you will want to combine all of the above – spiritual gifts, talents, and skills to help you pursue your passion and purpose. God uses these things together to create your story.

Your S. T. O. R. Y.

God works in all of these things to enable you to accomplish His will. I'm not the only person who believes this to be true. Best-selling author and one of my favorites, Max Lucado, shares in his book, *The Cure for the Common Life,* that we each have unique abilities and that no two of us are exactly alike. God has combined your specific gifts, talents, and skills to make you unique. As Lucado shares, we must know our own story in order to understand ourselves fully and truly know our purpose. Story, as Lucado explains, can be determined in five questions based on the acronym S.T.O.R.Y.

> S – What are your strengths? These are things you seem to have a knack for – organizing closets, solving problems, cooking a delicious meal.
>
> T – What is your topic? This refers specifically to what objects you enjoy using. Lucado gives the example of animals, statistics, or people. This is part of your passion. In Chapter Two, I asked you to make lists of the things that consumed your interest. Those objects are probably on that list. These are God-given fascinations. Pay attention to them.
>
> O – O is what Lucado calls optimal conditions. What motivates you? Some of us respond to needs, others respond to problems, while others thrive on order and routine. We work best in our optimal conditions.
>
> R – What about relationships? We are most satisfied when we relate to people in a way that makes us thrive. This may be in a team setting for some, while it could be one-on-one for others. Then there are those who prefer not to work with others at all but would rather work alone.

Y – Finally, the Y is Yes! When do you feel like shouting, "Yes!"? This is when you feel God's pleasure. When your story falls together perfectly, your strengths, topic, optimal conditions, and relationship patterns all come together correctly and you want to scream, "YES!" This is when you will live out your story. This is what Lucado calls your "sweet spot." When you live your story, you are in a prime position to sell your skills. [Max Lucado, Cure for the Common Life, Thomas Nelson, 2011]

You will be functioning at your prime and that will not only be valuable to you, but it will also be valuable to others. If you are, for example, someone who has the strength of organizing, your optimal condition is that, when you are solving someone's problem, you enjoy doing so one on one. You're in a situation where you can provide organizing services to others. Then you will be in a position to feel your YES! Because of this, you will do the job well and the person will be happy to pay you for your services.

This is why it is so important that you spend time discovering your talents, gifts, skills, and story. I read Lucado's book several years ago. At the time, I was attempting to discover my "sweet spot." I found this through my strengths of speaking and writing. I prefer to speak and write about my faith. My optimal condition is to teach or encourage others; these are my spiritual gifts. I also prefer to speak to groups of people. I feel my "YES!" when I am teaching through the written word or speaking to groups. I am able to do this both online and off by speaking, teaching workshops or sharing my written materials. I discuss this further in Chapter Eight.

This is what led me in 2008 to write the Christian Charm School materials. I knew that I was helping others and encouraging young girls. I was able to share one of my favorite topics, manners and etiquette, and able to do so with one of my strengths, writing.

It is worth taking the time to dig deep into each of these areas and discover what your strengths, optimal conditions, relationships, and topics are. Knowing these things, especially the relationship aspect, will help you in the next step, which we are about to cover: choosing your audience.

Chapter Seven

Choosing Your Audience

I held onto the microphone as best I could as my hands continued to shake. I had spoken in front of a group of people many times. I had been speaking since 2005, but this time was different. This time I was speaking to my peers. Women from across the United States had gathered for the first annual National Association of Christian Women Entrepreneurs conference in Dallas, Texas. It was April 2011. I was there to speak to those women about why information products should be a part of their business model. Choosing this audience was not something I ever thought I would do. Just five years prior to this conference, I didn't know what an information product was!

The audience I serve has changed over time. I want to begin this chapter by telling you that who you serve may change over time, too. There are many things you will want to consider when you're choosing whom you wish to serve.

Your audience, often called your niche or your target market, is essentially whom you wish to reach with your business. You won't necessarily have to stand before them and speak. As I mentioned previously, in today's marketplace we have more opportunity than ever to reach our own audiences, and to build a platform from which to speak to them.

It is essential that you know who your audience will be and that you understand them, their way of thinking, and their needs and problems. Obviously, every person is different; however, as humans, we all tend to have some things in common with others.

To determine who your audience will be, you might ask yourself the following questions:

- What age will my audience be?
- What will be the economic status of my audience?
- What is the education level of my audience?
- How will my audience like to take in information?

All of these questions will help you to obtain a better understanding of your audience. Let's explore why each of these things is important for you to know and understand.

Exploring Your Audience's Age

Different age groups think differently, have different needs, and communicate and gain knowledge in different ways. In order to meet the needs of, relate to, and truly connect with your audience, you need to know the general age group. Then you can prepare yourself to speak to, write for, or create a product or service for them.

If your audience is well-educated business women who want to escape the rat race, you would serve them differently than you would serve empty-nesters who want to find their purpose. In general, each age group has a different set of personal issues that you need to know as you prepare to share your passion with them and to serve them.

Exploring Your Audience's Economic Status

You may wonder why someone's economic status is of importance. Though it seems a bit harsh, it is relevant. If you are creating a book, workbook, or anything else that you hope to sell for profit, then you want to be sure that your audience has the funds with which to purchase that book. Likewise, if you hope to offer a service to a particular audience, you will need to know what they are willing and able to pay for such a service.

Either way, it is important to know your audience's economic status because it factors in and affects how you will reach them.

Exploring Your Audience's Education Level

Education brings another level of knowledge and understanding. This may affect how you communicate with your audience. There are many ways today to communicate; however, not everyone has the knowledge and understanding to take advantage of these ways. You may need to offer additional help or guidance to your audience if they do not have the knowledge needed to get the most out of what you offer.

An example could be for those of you who hope to create a community online or build a blog to minister to others. Maybe the audience you target isn't internet or technically savvy. What can you do to educate and assist them?

Education can factor in to how you will reach your particular audience. However, never allow a lack of a specific type of education on the part of your audience to get in your way. Instead, do all you can to assist them, because this is a part of serving them.

Meeting Your Audience's Needs/Solving Their Problems

The next thing that you need to consider regarding your audience is what you want to accomplish. Ultimately, you want either to meet a need or to solve a problem. In order to do so, you must first determine what that need or problem is. There are several ways to accomplish this. You can research your audience by connecting with them on social networks or by taking a poll or survey. Then you can make a list of the needs and problems they share. From this list you will create content or develop products and services to share with them. One wonderful idea is to share your first services or products for FREE. Yes, consider a free report, audio series, or video series to give away in exchange for their name and email address. This is called an "opt-in" offer and will help you to build a list, which is essential to business. Ultimately, your list will be your audience, because your goal will be to continue to build your list. Creating and building a list should be one of your first goals in business.

Once you know who your audience is and their most pressing need or biggest problem, you can seek to meet that need or solve that problem. You can begin to do so as soon as you create your first freebie. As I mentioned, this freebie can be written, or in audio or video form. Remember, different people learn in different ways, so consider the learning style of your audience as you create this product.

Just because this first content is going to be given away for free does not mean that you should not do your best work. To the contrary, you want your work to be top-notch and full of valuable information. You want to leave your potential client wanting more. You want to over-deliver and begin to establish a relationship with them.

Creating the content for this first project doesn't have to be difficult. Once you've discovered your audience's most pressing need or problem, you will want to address that need or problem. Consider, for example, that your audience is a homeschooling mother who can't complete her daily schedule. She wants to know how she can find more time in the day. You could create a short report or guide that would help her to create a working routine or schedule for herself and her family. This could include downloadable checklists that she can use to stay on track. Give the guide and checklist away for free on your website in exchange for her name and email address. This will begin to establish a relationship between the two of you.

You may be wondering, "Where do I find these people?" The answer is you go to where they are. If your target audience is homeschooling mothers, you learn where they meet online. I know there are thousands out there. In my research on homeschooling, I found dozens of online communities and followed a couple hundred homeschoolers on Twitter within a matter of a few days. These women will reach out to you if you reach out to them. The same is true for other niches as well. If you're not on Facebook and Twitter, you need to consider joining these two social media platforms.

I joined Twitter in 2007 before it was popular. Today, you can find just about any person, in any target market, on Twitter within a matter of minutes. The Twitter lists and search features will help you do this even faster.

You will also want to begin blogging with the same type of content for your niche, answering their questions, meeting their needs, and solving their problems. If you follow them on

Twitter and Facebook, you will begin to see the common questions or concerns that they, as a group, have in common and often ask. Then, you can begin to answer their questions through your blog posts. In addition, you will want to begin connecting with them by visiting their blogs and commenting on them. You will truly want to become a part of their community to establish the relationship with them that you seek. The key in the end is for them to know you, like you, and trust you. Until they do, they probably will not do business with you. Once you have these relationships established, you will want to begin proclaiming your message even louder. This next chapter gives you more ideas on how to do so.

Chapter Eight

Proclaiming Your Message

"I can do that," was a phrase I said often in the early days of my business. I learned quickly that if I didn't open my mouth and tell others about my business, no one else would do it for me.

As a young girl, I was super shy and hated drawing attention to myself. I would literally hide behind my mother. One of my speaking engagements was in my home church. A lady in the room, my piano teacher for a number of years, said before I began speaking, "Alyssa is the last person whom I ever expected to stand up in front of people and speak. She was the quietest child and I am so proud of her."

It is true that what I do today is not something I, or anyone around me, ever expected me to do. Following our passion and God's plan often leads us to unlikely places. Creating a platform from which to speak is what sharing our passion means.

Platform Building

A platform can mean a variety of things. Years ago, sharing one's message meant assembling others together, standing on a platform, and talking. There are now far more avenues by which to share one's message and passion with the world.

We will explore many of those avenues. It is important to remember with platform building that you are not building a tower, only a platform. Focus on just three of these things and do them well before trying others.

Creating a platform is creating marketing strategies for a business. As I mentioned, there are many avenues to accomplish this, and the good news is that many of these are low cost or no cost.

From the Ground Up

In 2005, when I began my speaking ministry, I was online but barely participating in anything remotely related to business. I knew next to nothing about business and marketing, but with the wave of the Internet and URLs flashing on almost every television commercial and billboard, I knew that having a website was a key ingredient to my success. Websites had become modern day business cards.

At that time, creating a website meant HTML and with my budget, I knew I would either have to learn it or hire someone to help me as the money became available. I found a graphic design student who created my first website in HTML because I agreed to be her guinea pig. Unfortunately, I learned quickly that I could not edit a single thing on that site. This was very frustrating. Fast forward another year. I discovered WordPress. This was also around the same time I quit my job to be home with my newborn daughter and preschool-age son. I used every spare moment to learn WordPress and to maintain my own website.

WordPress, though a blogging platform is a great way to obtain a highly functional, user friendly, search engine optimized website for your business. This is key, because a website is the foundation of your platform.

You must create a platform with four legs. It is important to start with only four, even though there are many options to choose from at first.

Choosing Your Four Legs of Marketing

The marketing legs to choose from include:

Social Media – We instantly receive a microphone from which to proclaim our message, thanks to social media. Social media is probably the fastest and easiest way to begin marketing your business, so we will start here. In it, there are what I consider the Big Four: Twitter, Facebook, Linked In, and YouTube. It is simple to get on each of these platforms. You sign up for an account, create a profile, and start posting. The key to social media is to be involved and consistent. Though it is possible to hire someone to handle social media for you, I don't recommend it. Social media is about networking and creating relationships, which can really only be done well personally

Blogging – Blogging is a form of social media which can take on a life of its own. I keep it separate because of its extensiveness and time commitment. It is an important piece of your website that can draw traffic, create community, and give you a stage from which to speak. Keeping up with a blog is time consuming, but worth the commitment. The keys to blogging include writing well, writing consistently, and promoting your blog via social media.

Article Writing – Once you become comfortable with writing, you can use article writing and marketing as a tool in your business. Article marketing can give a business owner a real advantage. The way it works is that a business owner writes an article on a topic relevant to her audience using key words that the audience would Google, to use a currently popular phrase. You would then submit those articles to article directories in the categories that are relevant to your audience. The article directories allow others to use your content under the provision that you receive credit for your article. Your credit is given in the form of a bio at the bottom of the article, which includes a link to your website or blog. Your bio is a key piece for you to do and do well. Create a bio that showcases your expert status and points to your website or blog.

The brilliance of article marketing is that we write one article and, by distributing it to article directories, we are able to multiply our efforts because the article is used again and again. The top article marketing directory is EzineArticles.com. I also recommend ArticleBin.com and for work-at-home, Wahm-articles.com.

Audios - For many of us, talking is much easier than writing. Many potential clients enjoy listening to a message more than they would reading it. With the popularity of IPods, IPhones, and IPads, people take their work on the go. Audios also give us another way by which to share our content. Once we write an article, we can use recording software to record ourselves speaking the same message, which gives a better return on our investment. Audios can easily become podcasts or even products such as downloadable mp3s, or physical CDs. There are also many opportunities on podcasts and radio shows to purchase audio ad space.

Radio/Interviews – Recording your own high quality audios can lead to opportunities to participate in other's radio shows or audio products, or to create your own. Often, if you put the word out, you can receive invitations to be on other people's online or offline radio shows or podcasts, or join them for teleseminars or audio conferences. You want to have recognition as the expert in your chosen field, and obtaining audio interviews and guest spots is a positive way to do so.

Information Products - Once you are comfortable sharing material, the next natural step is to create a product. Information products are a perfect fit for online business owners to create additional streams of income, and as a part of filling your funnel with potential clients and customers. They can also be a tool to use when building your first list.

Building a list is a key strategy to marketing a business. List building online consists of *giving* away something of value on our website in exchange for a person's name and email address. In most cases, the giveaway item is a free checklist, audio, ebook, special report, e-course, or something along those lines. This is your first step in creating a faithful follower who will begin to read your blog, receive your newsletter, and purchase your products, programs, or services. Chapter Eleven contains more information on building a faithful following online.

Press releases – When marketing a business, we probably all begin on a shoestring budget. Press releases are a cost-free way to promote your business using the local media. Press releases give information about your business. They usually need to have a particular slant or cause so that the reporters will bite on the story and do an article on you for the paper, or a piece on your local news channel.

I have utilized press releases a few times in my business. Each time, I found a press release template online and filled in the information to create something useable to send to the local press about my particular situation and myself. I have had news pieces and stories regarding my business or ministry in my hometown newspaper as well as a Christian publication. Both times, the stories had a slant that would be newsworthy. One of them focused on the ability to work from home that I had created for myself. The other focused on my mission of encouraging young girls to journal. Both times, the write-ups about me gave extensive information about myself and my business, as well as providing links to my website and my contact information.

Books – In today's society, becoming a published author is more and more reachable for the business owner. Many take advantage of the opportunity to self-publish and create their own business cards and/or their own book. It truly can catapult your business forward. I did this in 2007 by creating a workbook and leader guide called Christian Charm School for mothers or church or group leaders to use as a curriculum for teaching girls about biblical modesty and etiquette.

I had done workshops, which I called "Christian Charm School," in local churches. The workshops consisted of lessons on modesty, true beauty, speaking with confidence, proper posture and walk and dining etiquette. After receiving several phone calls and emails from those who saw the workshop availability on my website but were searching for written materials, which I hadn't yet created, I developed the workshop and leader guide. These sell on my website as both ebooks and in printed form. These still sell on a monthly basis, though I no longer focus on the girls' ministry as a part of my business.

Writing your first book doesn't have to mean a physical book. It can mean a workbook or even an ebook. Ebooks are becoming more and more popular with the use of Kindle, Nook and other e-readers. Also, ebooks are less costly to create.

Speaking - For many business owners, speaking may be a part of their business model already. For others, writing a book and creating a business can mean the need to explore speaking possibilities. A smart move for you as a business owner is to create a talk to share as a way of promoting yourself, your business, and perhaps any products you may have developed. Speaking may not come naturally for you, but it can be a valuable tool for your business.

The good news is that utilizing some of the things we've discussed, such as recording audios and being interviewed, can build your confidence in your ability to speak, and give you needed experience. You may want to obtain training in speaking as well. Most of all, it is important that you just get out and do it! Communicate and find speaking opportunities, which are more plentiful than you might think. Being willing to speak for free at first can lead to bigger opportunities, as well as paid ones, over time if you're patient.

The first time I spoke, I actually asked a friend if she would be my guinea pig group for presenting my Charm School material. She was a lay youth leader who didn't have a large budget and was happy to grant my request. She organized the event, arranged for there to be food, and had all the mothers and their daughters come to the church on a Friday evening to hear me present my materials. It was a hit, and I knew instantly I was doing what I was supposed to be doing.

Owning your own business means doing whatever it takes. It also means trusting the calling God gave you and the God who gave it to you. Let's talk seriously for a moment about what God does for us and what He expects of us in return.

Chapter Nine

Trusting in God's Miracle Math

"How much money do we have?" my husband asked. I cringed every time I heard those words. It was the end of the month, which meant the end of the money. In my years of working from home, I haven't always known where the money we needed would come from, but one thing I can tell you is that it has always come.

I like to call it God's miracle math. Our willingness to trust in God determines our ability to trudge through even our worst days. *We must put our trust in God, not in our ability to earn money.*

When I quit my salaried part-time job in ministry, I gave up a steady income. I quit in March and, by October, my family and I were feeling the pinch on our finances. I knew I had to do something, and God provided a way for me to make income from home with my writing in addition to the sporadic income I earned speaking.

Over the past four-plus years, my faith has increased as I have watched God provide for my family again and again. One of the keys to dealing with financial concerns is the realization that everything we have belongs to God.

What God's Word Says

God entrusts us with what He gives us - not only monetarily but also with our gifts and talents. That is why it is so important that we realize we have them and then use them.

This is why I focused on these things so heavily in the beginning of this book. Scripture tells us that, "From everyone who has been given much, much will be demanded; and from the one who has been entrusted with much, much more will be asked" (Luke 12:49 NIV).

We must use our talents, as well as our money, wisely and on a consistent schedule. God will bless us for what we choose to do with what He gives us. Recall the Parable of the Bags of Gold? Read it below:

"Again, it will be like a man going on a journey, who called his servants and entrusted his wealth to them. To one he gave five bags of gold, to another two bags, and to another one bag, each according to his ability. Then he went on his journey. The man who had received five bags of gold went at once and put his money to work and gained five bags more. So also, the one with two bags of gold gained two more. But the man who had received one bag went off, dug a hole in the ground and hid his master's money.

"After a long time the master of those servants returned and settled accounts with them. The man who had received five bags of gold brought the other five.

'Master,' he said, 'you entrusted me with five bags of gold. See, I have gained five more.'

"His master replied, 'Well done, good and faithful servant! You have been faithful with a few things; I will put you in charge of many things. Come and share your master's happiness!'

"The man with two bags of gold also came. 'Master,' he said, 'you entrusted me with two bags of gold; see, I have gained two more.'

"His master replied, 'Well done, good and faithful servant! You have been faithful with a few things; I will put you in charge of many things. Come and share your master's happiness!'

"Then the man who had received one bag of gold came. 'Master,' he said, 'I knew that you are a hard man, harvesting where you have not sown and gathering where you have not scattered seed. So I was afraid and went out and hid your gold in the ground. See, here is what belongs to you.'

"His master replied, 'You wicked, lazy servant! So you knew that I harvest where I have not sown and gather where I have not scattered seed? Well then, you should have put my money on deposit with the bankers, so that when I returned I would have received it back with interest.

"'So take the bag of gold from him and give it to the one who has ten bags. For whoever has will be given more and they will have an abundance. Whoever does not have, even what they have will be taken from them. And throw that worthless servant outside, into the darkness, where there will be weeping and gnashing of teeth." (Matthew 25:14-20 NIV)

This story helps us to see clearly that God is faithful and His blessings are abundant when we are faithful to Him and with the blessings that He has given us. He also promises, "As

I was with Moses, so I will be with you; I will **never leave** you nor forsake you" (Joshua 1:5 NIV, emphasis mine). These words are actually found in Scripture multiple times. Our Lord wants us to know that He will take care of us.

If you are not already aware of God's faithfulness, learn to trust in it. He will not fail you. Knowing this, you need to be willing to give back to Him because He has given so much to you. One way that you may want to do this is through tithing.

The Tithe

I will admit that this was a struggle for me in my early years of marriage. Although I'm sure my mother and father tithed, it wasn't something that they taught us to do. We would give a dollar here or there in Sunday school or in the offering plate, but I do not recall a specific conversation on the meaning of tithing or how it worked.

My education on tithing came from the school of hard knocks. Early in my marriage, I was determined to do well with our finances. Despite my best efforts, I still struggled. One of the common questions that I was asked was, "Do you tithe?" Every person who told me this backed up his or her question with the loving advice, "You cannot out-give God." They assured me that God would bless my efforts.

Soon, my husband and I began to tithe. I can recall many times when I would write out my tithe check, lay it in the offering plate, and say a prayer that I would have enough money for the other needs we had that week. Each time, not only did we have the money, but many, many times, God blessed us with even more. A new client would appear, someone would gift us with a few dollars here or there, or maybe someone would bring us food or items that we needed "just because."

We have had blessings such as a church member who gave us a gigantic garbage bag full of a variety of sizes of diapers. At the time we had two babies in diapers.

God shows up in big ways and small ways for us and He will do the same for you, when you are obedient to Him and what His Word teaches. His Word teaches us to tithe.

To tithe means to give back a tenth of what He has given to us. As part of trusting God, we must learn to give back our tenth. This means if we make $100, we should give $10 back to God. When we tithe, I believe we should tithe to the local church. I hope you are a part of a church family where you can give your tithe.

Some of us are called to give above and beyond a tithe. This is an offering.

My husband and I have given offerings for special funds that are collected in the church. Many times this may be done for help with disaster relief, church planting projects, mission trips, or other specific ministries.

An offering is, of course, optional. Either way, when we give to the Lord, we will see results. The Lord is clear that He loves a cheerful giver and that he will bless us abundantly for our obedience to His commands.

"Give, and it will be given to you. A good measure, pressed down, shaken together and running over, will be poured into your lap. For with the measure you use, it will be measured to you" (Luke 6:38 NIV).

Though I have been the receiver of God's blessings and I have often done the hard things to follow His Word, this does not mean that I have done so without trembling at times.

Calm My Anxious Heart

I sat in the college parking lot and hurriedly dialed the automatic teller to my bank. I fumbled to punch in my bank account number and pin. The automated voice came on the line saying, "Your account balance is negative six dollars and six cents." My heart sank and a clog formed in my throat. Tears stung my eyes as I realized what had happened. This was the first time in our young marriage that this had happened. Furiously, I dialed my husband's number. Terrified of what his reaction might be, through my sobs I explained to him what had happened. "It's not that big of a deal, Alyssa," he said calmly. "It happens to people every day. It could be worse, and I get paid tomorrow."

My husband has always been a calm and levelheaded constant in my life. My anxiety levels can soar and then bottom out within a matter of minutes, but my husband can level out the playing field with ease.

Early in my marriage, while I was still in college, my husband supported us on his salary. Three to five days a week, I would make the seventy mile each way trip to college for classes and back home. For months, I had been listening to a money guy on talk radio who just happened to come on the radio every day at the time I was on my way home.

You may have heard of the famous Dave Ramsey. Dave shared with guest after guest his tried and true plan for financial peace. As a young newlywed, I truly wanted to live a debt-free lifestyle. One day I even called the show and Dave generously sent me a copy of his first book, *Financial Peace,* as a late wedding gift.

I began to create a written budget for our finances as a result of Dave's teachings. Most months, even recent months in our life, I have looked at it and thought we would end up with more month left than money. Though I cannot tell you how, other than God's provision, we always made it through the month with our bills paid and our stomachs full.

Unfortunately, we have created some debt over the last twelve years, as three babies were born; we built a house, and purchased a minivan. Of course, there were also medical bills, private school tuition, and other decisions that have caused us to pay what Dave would call "stupid tax." Now, we're in the process of getting out of debt. I believe that, as a Christian mom who is also a business owner, it is imperative that all areas of our lives be in line with Scripture, which tells us "the borrower is slave to the lender" (Proverbs 22:7 NIV). Therefore, we must choose to get out of debt.

Get Rid of Debt

I wish my husband and I could have avoided debt. I am a Christian and my debts from the past weigh heavy on my heart. Having a good portion of our income each month go to paying debt is disheartening, but I want to be faithful in paying off our debts. If you and your family do not currently have debt, please do not make the mistake of funding your business through debt. It is not worth it, and I do not recommend doing so. A thriving, God-honoring business can be created on a shoestring. It all comes by building your brand.

Chapter Ten

Building Your Brand

"Branding" is a common term in the business world today. We probably know more about it than we realize, yet as work-at-home entrepreneurs, we wonder if it is something we should do. If so, what is the cost? Also, do we begin the process simultaneously with the start of our business, or later? All these questions have run through my mind as I've built a business over the last five years.

You probably know more about branding than you realize. Think about it for a moment. What immediately comes to mind when I say, "McDonalds"? The golden arches, right?

What if I said, "Nike"?. . . "The swoosh!"

Or . . . "Burger King"? . . . "Have it Your Way!" or that scary King character they have now.

Branding is simply something that will remind others of you. Recently I attempted to change the branding I used for years. Not only were my clients confused, I felt as if I was trying to wear someone else's clothes. On a visit to my mother's house, I had an accident that required a change of clothing. She loaned me some clothes to wear home. I felt strange. They smelled like her; they looked like her. I love my mother, but her clothes just didn't look like me.

The same is true for your **BRAND.** You want it to reflect YOU. You are the starting piece of your brand. I have new entrepreneurs ask me WHEN they should brand themselves, whether early--before they have a website, a Facebook fan page, etc. -- or later. My answer is that your brand is your starting point, your foundation, and the basis for your business. Only YOU can tell others who you really are and only YOU can give an accurate description of your business. You can hire a graphic designer to create a logo, or a website designer to create your website, but only YOU can determine the foundation of your brand.

You have to be comfortable with your brand and make sure it reflects you before you share it with others. So, yes, the branding step of business would come before you put up a website or a Facebook fan page, unless you want to spend unnecessary money to redo it.

Another woman asks how she could know her brand. She says, *"I used to brand myself as a ghostwriter (is that really a "brand" anyway? Or just a "title" or "label"?) But I'm not doing that anymore. I'm writing for God now, not others. When it comes to Mending Hope, I think of myself as one who writes to encourage women in their relationship with God. Does any of that make sense? When I hear the word "brand" I automatically think brand=image (i.e. the golden arches=McDonald's brand). But I can't wrap my brain around applying that concept to myself."* Hope Wilbanks, http://mendinghope.com

Yes, Hope, that makes absolute sense and I'm sure others ask the same question. Actually, I have asked myself this same question many times, because my goal was to pursue my passion and purpose. I believe we can brand ourselves and still do that. In today's marketplace, with the use of social media, we can brand ourselves. And the truth is, we can more easily brand ourselves and make ourselves recognizable than some large companies can with the big budgets and endless resources. People connect most easily with other people, and by putting your smiling face and amazing personality out there to connect with others, you can establish a likeable brand easily. You will want your brand to reflect you. What makes people notice you? What motivates you? Use those things to establish your brand.

Ever since I was a little girl, purple has been my favorite color. I chose it as a part of my brand, originally, because I was targeting teen and tween girls and their mothers, and the color seemed feminine. I chose to keep the color purple as a part of my brand because of its "regal" factor. It looks professional and clean paired with white and grays, as I have chosen to use it. I also use feminine fonts because I'm targeting women, and we like the look and feel that these fonts bring.

I also encourage my clients to use their own beautiful face as a part of their brand because of the ability it gives to connect with other people. This is why using videos in your marketing can be so appealing to your audience.

Let us now discuss the issue that troubles Hope. Is branding creating a label? I don't believe so. I see branding as your tagline and image, which help make your mission possible. These things work together to make you recognizable in the marketplace.

For example, my mission is: "Guiding Christian moms in their pursuit of passion, purpose and profits." I often use the tag line: "passion, purpose and profits." My image is the gorgeous purple and pretty script-like fonts. I also consider the clean look of my website to be a part of my brand.

However, my label or title is author, speaker, strategist and mom entrepreneur. I don't consider this part of my brand as much as my title.

The <u>American Marketing Association</u> defines **brand** as a "name, term, design, symbol, or any other feature that identifies one seller's goods or services as distinct from those of other sellers. The legal term for brand is trademark."

You want to trademark you and your business. One reason this can be difficult for many moms is they do not realize the value that their brand has in their business. We must realize first of all that we ourselves are valuable and that the talents, gifts, and abilities that we have to share with the world are worth branding and sharing.

I believe that investment is part of people's hesitation about branding. This was a big hesitation for me because having graphics created and setting up a website required a monetary investment. One of the positives is that, most of the time, this is a one-time investment or set up cost that will provide a return on your investment for years to come. It is important, therefore, that you present your best self.

Presenting Your Best Self

Presentation is key in branding. We want to present our best selves. Always remember, everything that we present must be at a professional level. A drawback of the Internet is that if you put information on it, it stays there. The Internet is forever, and you only get one chance to make that first impression on your potential clients and customers.

Remember, your brand's basic pieces are your logo or graphics, including the colors and fonts, your slogan or tagline, and your mission statement. Take your time creating these pieces. This is a fun part of business set-up and should be one of the first investments you make in your business. Be willing to take the risk, spend the money, and invest in your business.

Though this is the first step, there will be many steps along the way that will help you to maintain your brand. That's why it's important to remember that this, and other parts of your business as well, are a process. It's a cliché, but bears repeating: Rome wasn't built in a day and your business won't be either. Take things step-by-step. What's important is that you start.

Chapter Eleven

Just Do It, Do It Again

You are at the beginning of a long journey of faith. In order to endure the journey, you must be prepared. Just as athletes train for their sports continually, you must train for this journey continually. You must not stop. You must continue.

As the Bible says, *"Do you not know that in a race all the runners run, but only one gets the prize? Run in such a way as to get the prize. Everyone who competes in the games goes into strict **training**. They do it to get a crown that will not last; but we do it to get a crown that will last forever"* (1 Corinthians 9:24-25 NIV emphasis mine).

Training is necessary for all of us regardless of how big or small our leap of faith seems. If we are called to this by God, then we must be committed to Him and discipline ourselves to daily training. There are some essentials for those of us committed to the task of doing the work God has called us to do. These essentials are: prayer, studying God's Word, and being committed to other spiritual disciplines. Let's explore these essentials.

Prayer

Prayer is our communication with God, our Father. We should learn from the perfect example of Jesus, who often retreated to be alone to pray. He made spending time with the Father His priority. If the only perfect man who ever lived spent time with God daily in prayer, why should we think that we, as imperfect humans, should be able to do it all on our own?

It is important to commit to a specific time of day to pray. Many times if you do not plan your prayer time, it will quickly fall by the wayside and you will not do it. Committing yourself to pray is important. Find that time alone for conversation with God. It will equip you for all the other tasks you will have to do each day.

Studying God's Word

God's Word gives us direction, pierces our hearts, and shows us where we need to add to or take away from our lives. It is the ultimate decision-maker when we need to find answers, and will inspire us when we need encouragement.

As Christians taking on the overwhelming task of choosing to work from home, there is so much we can glean from the Bible. Therefore we must make it a priority to study and know it. God's words also apply to those areas of our lives with which we all struggle. Being committed to the reading and studying of God's Word is truly an essential part of our lives.

Other Spiritual Disciplines

Because I realize we may not all have the same religious traditions and disciplines, I will preface this section by saying that these disciplines may not apply to your situation, but in my Southern Baptist faith the following are ones that I practice. As people committed to God, there should be disciplines we all practice in that commitment to Him. Some of these include:

Tithing - Giving back to God is an important discipline for us as Christians. The Bible tells us to give back a tenth of our first fruits to the Lord. Tithing is a discipline that, when practiced, will result in many blessings from God. Remember, God loves a "cheerful" giver. We talked extensively about tithing in Chapter Nine.

Keeping of the Sabbath - When God created the earth, He took the seventh day to rest. We are also called to a day of rest. This is known as the Sabbath day and is a day we should be free from work and able to rest and recoup from the week, preparing our minds and hearts for the week ahead.

Some Important Relationships - In addition to the above-named essentials, we want to have certain people in our life. As an old poem states, "No man is an island." We were created to work together and to support each other in the faith. That is why we want to be sure and have the following people by our side:

An accountability partner - What does being accountable mean? When we are held accountable, we are "subject to explanation." We must, therefore, explain our actions. We can be held accountable not only for our actions and sins, but for those things we are NOT doing. We can have our accountability partner hold us accountable for the "essentials" we discussed earlier. Whatever the accountability partners agree upon is between them.

In order to be held accountable, we must be willing to be honest and responsible for our actions. It may sound a bit scary. A relationship with someone who we can trust, and who will hold us accountable, is personal. It is also a great way to make certain we practice the essentials and avoid the things that would keep us from doing so. When looking for an accountability partner it is important to look for someone who is:

A. Close to your age – This does not necessarily mean chronological age, but could also mean "maturity" level. People mature at different speeds and you'll want to consider "Christian" maturity as well. You will need to be on the same level with this person.

B. Trustworthy - You will need to be able to discuss personal issues with the person and know that person will keep them confidential.

C. Shares the same morals and beliefs - In order to be able to hold each other accountable, you must have the same morals and beliefs. If you don't believe in drinking alcoholic beverages, but your accountability partner does, you won't be able to hold that person accountable in that area.

Over the years, I have had numerous accountability partners who came into my life at different times, but each at just the right time. They were there to pray for me and pick me up when I needed it. An accountability partner has always been a key person in my life.

A Mentor - It is important to have someone who we can look to when we need some advice, a shoulder to cry on, or a sounding board to discuss ideas. A mentor is different from an accountability partner in that, in most cases, the person has more experience in our field. This does not mean that they are older than us, though this may be the case. They will, however, have the knowledge and experience that we lack. Whether we choose a Godly woman of faith, an experienced work-at-home mom, or a person experienced in our chosen field, we need to choose the type of mentor we feel will be most beneficial to our needs.

I have always chosen people as mentors who were successful in the things that interested me. This helped me to learn how they had reached the success I wanted to experience.

Again, as with the accountability partner, you will want to choose someone you can trust. You will also want to determine how you will work together with your mentor. Talk with them and see what they feel comfortable doing. Having a mentoring relationship can take on many forms. Just decide between the two of you if you want to meet weekly, monthly or not in person at all. Will you communicate via telephone, email or only face-to-face? Will you plan activities to do together, or will you just "wing it"? The whole process can be a learning and growing experience for both of you.

These essentials and people are important to have by your side. They will help keep your project running like a well-oiled machine. You will surely realize that if you skip any of these essentials in your daily walk, something about your days will not go well. When you take a leap of faith, you truly put your life in God's hands and, therefore, you must consult with Him regularly to be sure you are on the proper path.

As you continue on this journey, you will be excited about the possibilities and the many things that happen. If God truly has called you to this journey, you will begin to see Him open doors only He can open.

Anytime you question these opportunities, ask Him in prayer and He will show you the way. Remember, He can open, but also shut doors that only He can close.

If you are like me, you will now want to begin sharing your exciting journey with others. Doing so is also a great way to promote your mission. The following is a helpful way to reach out to others and inform them about your journey. You never know what their connections might bring about for you.

Reach Out

Begin by making a list that contains the following people:
Old Friends – include those from high school, college, and previous jobs.
Family – Think beyond immediate family into extended family.
Colleagues/Acquaintances – Anyone who you come in contact with on a regular basis.

Next, you will want to write a letter or send an email. This can be one letter which you copy and send to all of those on your list, explaining your leap of faith, your mission, and what you hope to accomplish. You can then ask them to pray for you, as well as ask for referrals. Just share your joy, your experience, and your journey with them. This will be a great way to get the word out and it will help you make the connections that you need to make. As a speaker, you can get bookings. As someone in business, you can make connections to opportunities. No matter what else you may accomplish, by sharing with others what God is doing in your life you can never go wrong. To avoid making it sound like a form letter, you should alter each to include something personal to that person.

Let us summarize the many different ways that you can prepare for your journey. Use the following checklist to make a plan of preparation.

<u>Checklist</u>
- o   Set a time for prayer and Bible Study each day.
- o   Locate an accountability partner.
- o   Locate a mentor.
- o   Establish a prayer team.
- o   Make a list of people you know.

o   Write a letter and send it to those people.

Why are you waiting? Take that leap of faith and get started on your journey to passion, purpose, and profits!

SOURCES

Books

John Ortberg, *If You Want to Walk on Water*, Grand Rapids, MI: Zondervan, 2001, 17

Francis Chan, *Crazy Love*, David C. Cook, 2008

Florence Littauer, *Personality Plus*, Revell; Revised and Expanded edition, 1992

Florence Littauer, *Your Personality Tree,* Thomas Nelson, 1989

Dave Ramsey, *Financial Peace*, Lampo; 2002

John Maxwell, *Today Matters*, Center Street, 2005

Max Lucado, *Cure for the Common Life*, Thomas Nelson, 2011

Websites

http://www.gotoquiz.com/personality_plus_1

http://www.churchgrowth.org/analysis/intro.php

http://christiejarvis.com

http://newlifebalanceforwomen.com

http://ThePeacefulHousewife.com

http://mendinghope.com

http://amainsights.com/

About the Author

Alyssa Avant is an author, speaker, strategist and mom entrepreneur. Alyssa has been working virtually since 2007. She has years of experience working with online professionals and business owners. Alyssa has also been published in the Inspired Women Succeed book, in numerous magazines, on various websites, and is the author and creator of Christian Charm School Workbook materials.

Alyssa is a former youth and children's director who spent over 5 years ministering to youth and speaking to teen and tween girls on the issues of modesty, beauty and being a Godly girl. Alyssa still volunteers as the youth and children's activities director at the church she and her family attend regularly.

She is driven to help others. She knows there are other moms who have felt or feel just like she did in the early days of building a profitable business amidst the craziness of kids and on a budget. She desires to share her knowledge with YOU and help YOU not to make the mistakes she did.

Today, everything she does, from Do-It-Yourself Programs to Webinars, is about helping mom business owners move ahead in business with practical tools on a budget while staying home with their children.

Alyssa holds her Bachelors degree in Psychology from the University of Mississippi, and is pursuing her Master's in Christian Leadership from Liberty Baptist Theological Seminary.

She is an avid social media marketer, loves Coca Cola Classic, Jesus, her husband, and three precious children (not in that order). She and her family reside in Carrollton, Mississippi.